Origins

Cuckoo Trouble

Tony Bradman ✳ Jonatronix

OXFORD
UNIVERSITY PRESS

Previously...

In the story *Underwater Adventure*, Tiger drops his watch in the pond in the park, after a scare from Cat.

Max and Ant reveal their latest invention – a Super Micro-Submarine. Max says that they will be able to use it to rescue Tiger's watch.

Max and Ant set off on an underwater adventure. They are chased by water-beetle larvae and have to hide in some weeds to escape.

Ant spots Tiger's watch but when they try to get it the engine breaks down. They are stuck. Max contacts Cat and Tiger and asks them to find a spare part for the submarine. Tiger has a crazy idea …

4

Chapter 1 – Tiger's plan

"Let go of me, Tiger!" Cat said. She stopped on the path. "I'm not taking another step until you tell me what you're up to!"

"We're going to my house! My dad's bought a cuckoo clock … come on!"

Tiger grabbed Cat's hand again and pulled her, but she dug her heels in.

"Wait, Tiger!" Cat said. "I don't understand. Explain your plan properly or I won't know how to help!"

Tiger took a deep breath and told her about his dad's new cuckoo clock. He thought it might contain the clockwork part that would save Max and Ant.

"We'll need to shrink to climb inside it," he said. "That's why I need you with me. My watch is at the bottom of the pond, remember? You'll have to shrink me, too."

"Why didn't you say that in the first place?" asked Cat.

She turned and ran off. Tiger shook his head and raced after her.

Soon they arrived at Tiger's house. They peered in through a window and saw his mum and dad. They were sitting in the front room watching TV.

"Oh, no!" whispered Tiger. "The clock is on the wall behind them."

"We can't let them see us," said Cat.

There was only one thing for it. Tiger held Cat's arm. She turned the dial on her watch and …

Chapter 2 – Climbing a mountain

Cat and Tiger ran round to the back door. They used the cat flap to get inside. Luckily Tiger's cat, Moggy, was not around. They headed for the front room.

Cat and Tiger sprinted behind the sofa. Tiger's mum and dad were too busy watching TV to notice.

Quickly, they crossed the carpet until they were right underneath the clock. Cat stared up.

"How are we going to get up there?" she asked. "It's as high as a mountain!"

Tiger hadn't thought of that. He looked round the room hoping to get an idea. Then he spotted a piece of wool that Moggy had been playing with.

"I know," he said. He ran over to the wool, picked it up and slung it over his shoulder. "We can climb up the bookcase and then swing across to the clock using the wool like a rope!"

Cat looked unsure.

"Trust me, Cat. It will be fine ..."

Soon, they were climbing up the bookcase.

When they got to the third shelf, Cat made the mistake of looking down. She gasped as she felt her head begin to spin. Tiger quickly reached out and grabbed her arm, pulling her to safety.

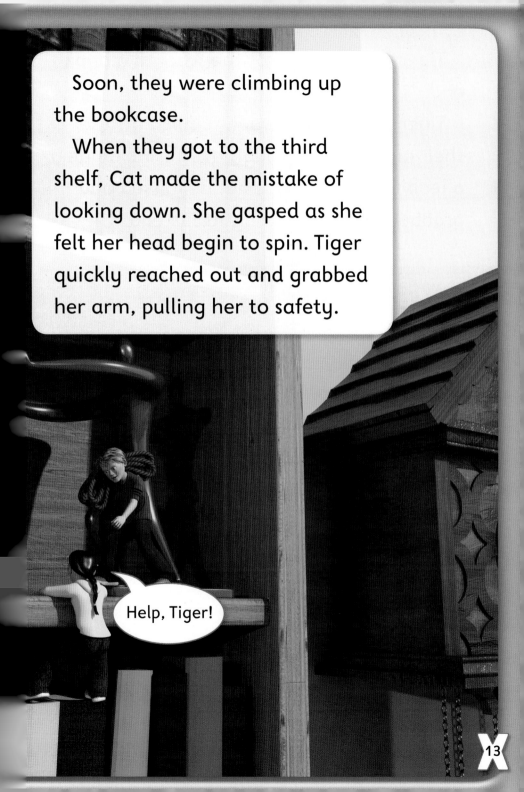

Help, Tiger!

Tiger tied one end of the wool to a book end. "I'll go first," he said.

Tiger gripped the wool, jumped off the shelf and swung through the air. He made a leap for the clock ... but he missed and grabbed one of the weights instead.

Cat forgot her own fear.
"Hold on, Tiger!" she
yelled. "I'll save you!"
Cat pulled the wool
back in. She held on tight
and swung out towards
the clock. She landed on
another weight.

That made Tiger's weight
shoot upwards inside
the clock. As soon as
Tiger jumped off the
weight, Cat shot
upwards, too.
"What a wild
ride!" said Cat, as
she leapt off.
Now, they
were both inside
the clock …

Chapter 3 – A deathly hush

The air smelt of wood and machine grease. Cat and Tiger stared open-mouthed at all the brass cogs and wheels that spun round and round. Shiny levers clicked up and down and there was a loud tick-tick-ticking. Everything seemed to be moving at once.

"Come on," said Tiger, finally. "We've got to get back to Max and Ant."

The two friends made their way through the inside of the clock. They clambered over and under the clockwork pieces, looking for the part that Max had described. They finally found the bit they were looking for.

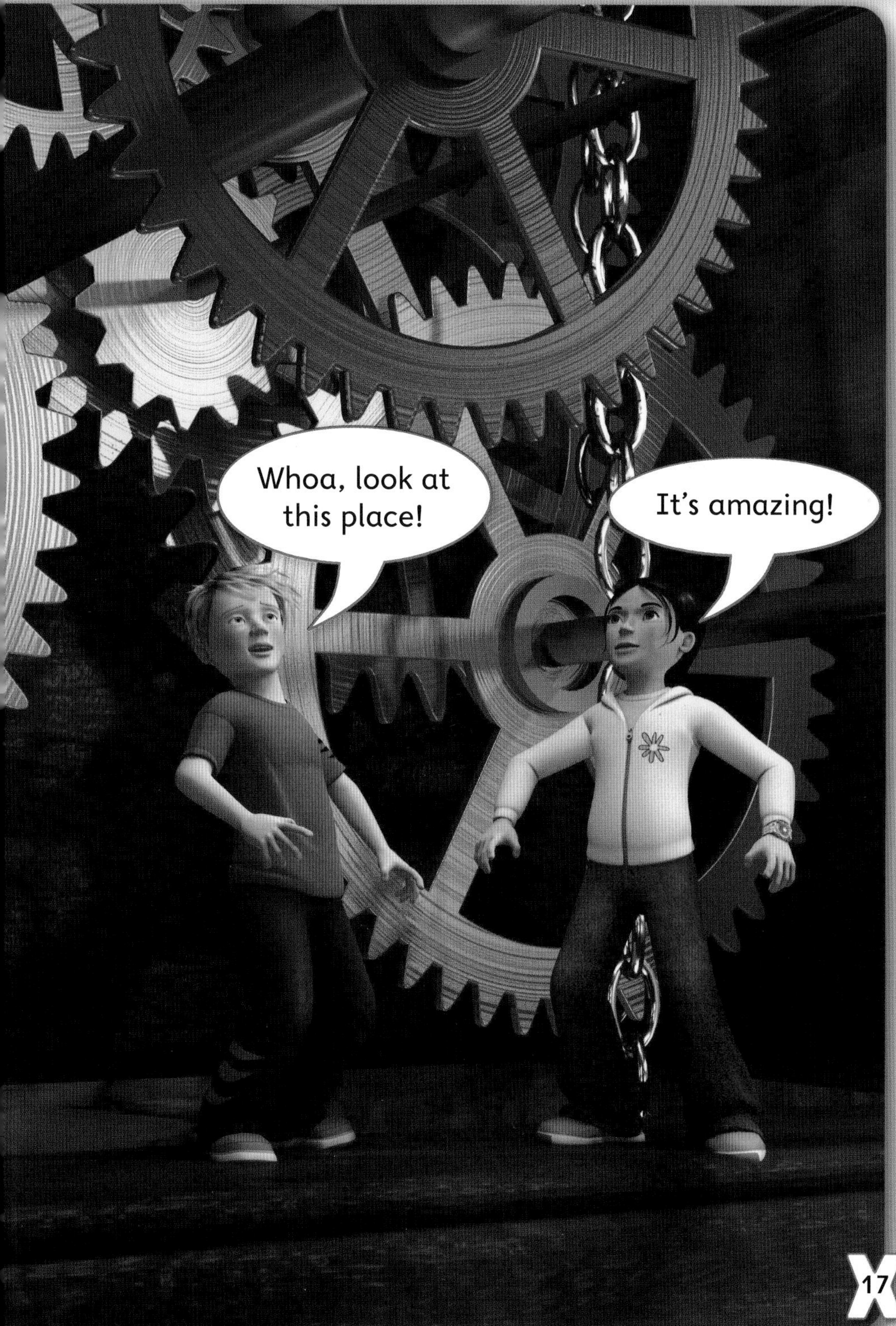
Whoa, look at this place!
It's amazing!

"What now?" said Cat.

"We'll have to get it off," said Tiger. "Give me a hand."

Tiger took one side, Cat the other. They began to pull the cog off. After a while Cat paused. She seemed puzzled.

"Is it my imagination or has it gone very quiet in here?" she said.

Tiger listened. It was true. All the ticking and whirring had stopped. A deathly hush had settled over the clock.

Then there was a loud *BOINNNNNGGGG!* and a huge, dark shape rushed out of the darkness and crashed straight into Tiger …

Meanwhile, back underwater ...

   THUMP! The water-beetle larvae had found the submarine. They were trying to break in again. They had made a dent in the outside of the craft. Max checked the periscope. There was still no sign of Cat or Tiger.

I don't think we can take much more of this!

Chapter 4 – Twelve o'clock shock

Tiger was flung backwards. He had no choice but to hang on. He flew out of the clock like a rocket being launched.

Then he heard another loud noise … *CUCKOO!*

"Help!" he yelled, as the spring holding the cuckoo snapped back.

Cat made a grab for him, but he was going too quickly. *BOINNNNGGG!* Tiger shot out again.

"Just hold on!" shouted Cat. "It's only marking the hour. It will stop, err … eventually."

"Eventually?" yelled Tiger, panicking. "Why, what time is it?"

"Twelve o'clock," said Cat.

BOINNGG, CUCKOO! BOINNGG, CUCKOO!

Tiger groaned. He was beginning to feel sick. He was just thankful that the TV was turned up loud so that his mum and dad didn't hear him yelling.

Finally there was one last *BOINNGG, CUCKOO!* His ordeal was over.

Tiger felt shaky as he let go of the cuckoo.

"Let's get out of here before anything else goes wrong," he said.

Together they pulled the cog free. Tiger tied the cog to the wool and lowered it to the ground. Then he tied the other end of the wool to a hook in the clock. Cat climbed down first, followed by Tiger. He only hoped Max and Ant were still OK …

Chapter 5 – Rod and line

There was another thump against the side of the submarine. The metal creaked and groaned as the water-beetle larvae hit it.

"Oh, no!" gasped Ant, feeling a drip on his head. "We've sprung a leak!"

It was not a big leak yet. But the submarine wouldn't hold out much longer.

Max looked again through the periscope.
To his delight he saw Cat and Tiger running
towards the edge of the pond. Cat was
waving frantically. Tiger was pointing to
something in his hand.

"They're back," cried Max, in relief.

"Thank goodness!" said Ant.

"How are we going to get the cog to them?" asked Cat.

"I've already thought of that," said Tiger.

There were some boys fishing nearby. Tiger ran over to them and borrowed a spare rod and line. He put the cog on the hook and cast it into the water.

Max and Ant heard the cog clatter against the periscope. The noise scared the water-beetle larvae away.

"It's a good job Tiger's such a good shot!" said Ant.

They saw the cog sink down in the water, past the front of the submarine. Quickly, Max turned the two handles that operated the grabbing claws at the front of the submarine.

Max guided the grabbing claws, now holding the spare cog, towards the airlock. Soon the cog was safely inside the submarine. Then he and Ant fitted it to the engine.

"Try it now, Ant," Max said at last.

Ant began to pedal and the engine came to life. Max and Ant smiled.

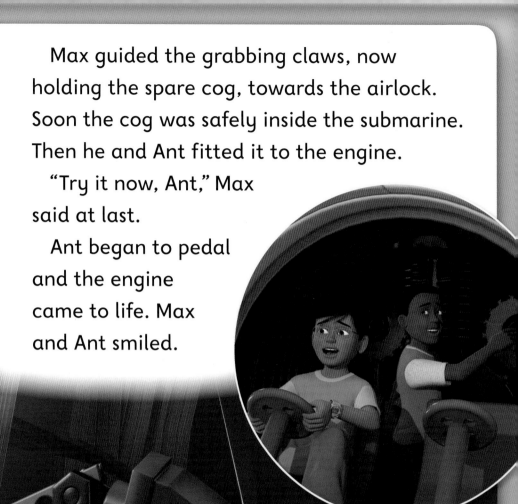

Max and Ant picked up Tiger's watch with the grabbing claws. Then they steered the submarine to the surface.

When they were back on dry land, Max gave Tiger his watch and the cog back. Tiger grabbed them and began to run.

"Hey, where are you going?" shouted Max.

Tiger didn't answer. He had to get home and put the cog back before his dad discovered there was something wrong with his antique cuckoo clock!

Sometimes Tiger wished his life could be just a little easier …

Find out more ...

Find out more about **Inventors and Inventions** in *Flying Machines ...*

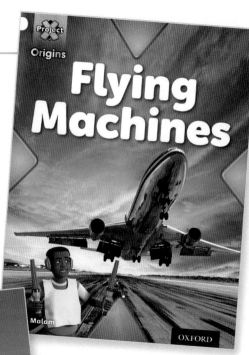

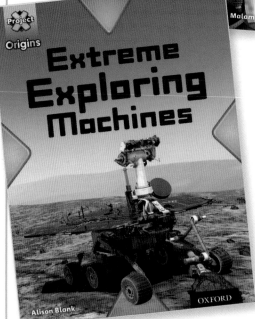

and *Extreme Exploring Machines.*